WHERE THE MOUNTAINS WERE

edited by
Rowan Beckett Minor
and Joshua Gage

Where the Mountains Were

First Printing

ISBN 978-1-7350257-9-7

Cover design and image courtesy of The Befuddled Press.

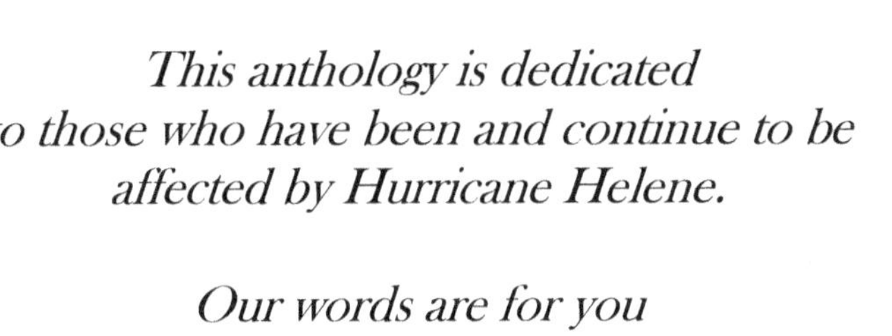

*This anthology is dedicated
to those who have been and continue to be
affected by Hurricane Helene.*

*Our words are for you
and our hearts are with you.*

INTRODUCTION

no heat
to keep us warm
darkening sky

For those who don't know me well, I've had to move around quite a bit. I was born in West Virginia and Appalachia is my home, but I spent most of my years living in various towns in North Carolina. Growing up in both the Coastal Plain and Piedmont regions, I have both evacuated for and hunkered down in many hurricanes, the earliest I remember being Fran in '96. It's been a long time since I've personally seen this level of destruction from a hurricane, and never in my life have I seen the Appalachian region affected this badly from a hurricane. The Mountains of North Carolina are also a special place I hold in my heart. Boone, NC was the first place I lived on my own and

Tweetsie Railroad was my first real job. I have several family and friends who live in Western NC, some affected by Helene, so it is an understatement to say I have felt small and useless.

One morning after Helene made landfall, I was a devastated mess when Joshua reminded me to use my platforms and do what I'm good at. After some discussions, we decided it would be best to co-edit a disaster relief haiku anthology and all proceeds would go to a local organization in Western NC. So, we took to social media and rallied for haiku on the themes of storms and natural disasters. With such a quick turn around, we were just hoping to get enough submissions for the anthology to make, but our community came through and within a few short weeks, we had over 130 submissions.

This anthology, which contains 100 haiku and senryu by over 60 poets, features poems by several people who know folks affected by Helene, who were affected themselves by Helene, or who were affected by another severe storm. Joshua and I are sincerely thankful to everyone who lent their poems and personal experiences for the making of *Where the Mountains Were*. This anthology would not exist without you and we are forever grateful that you came together with us to support all of those who have been and continue to be affected by Hurricane Helene. Community is needed more now than ever, and empathy is one of our greatest tools for survival.

Rowan Beckett Minor
December 1, 2024

WHERE THE MOUNTAINS WERE

SAM CALHOUN

no red sky
while the cardinal sings
storms are coming

ROBERTA BEACH JACOBSON

local weather map
tv meteorologist
points to my town

ting a snake skin off the bramble tornado watch

FRANK HIGGINS

tornado warning
moths swirling at noon
around the streetlight

RICH SCHILLING

storm clouds
what a father says
with silence

DYLAN STOVER

kettle whine—
the rising fists
of horizon cumulus

EAVONKA ETTINGER

storm warning
the emergency kit
we never made

VALORIE BROADHURST WOERDEHOFF

tornado warning
exes and new spouses
share a basement

ERIN CASTALDI

midnight storm watch three fingers of scotch

BEN GAA

cicadas
tornado sirens
cicadas

DYLAN STOVER

until it isn't red dawn

NITU YUMNAM

evacuation
the last look
at everything

ERIN CASTALDI

hen everything turns silhouette funnel clouds

BECKA CHESTER

one red dragonfly
the tornado far from here
still terrifies me

KENDALL LOTT

rolling thunder
she reaches for her
dolly's hand

JULIE BLOSS KELSEY

the choice to hide
in doorway or bathtub—
yellow-green sky

MICHELE ROOT-BERNSTEIN

howling wind
an urge to print my hand
upon the wall

REID HEPWORTH

thunderstorm
the dog hightails it
back to bed

DAN SCHWERIN

when to stop the cloud never gets clear

MICHAEL HENRY LEE

raging river
a cicada husk clings to
the screened porch door

ALLYSON WHIPPLE

midnight storm
the flowers all shaken
off my hibiscus

BRYAN RICKERT

frozen winds
howling all night long
the neighbor's hound

VALENTINA RANALDI-ADAMS

25

power outage—
celebrating mass
by candlelight

JOHN PAPPAS

nor'easter
again she counts
the candles

EAVONKA ETTINGER

caught in snow
a frazzled state tries
to find a plow

DEBBIE STRANGE

storm hour
the cliff's face carved
a little deeper

JOHN PAPPAS

snowblind
the white-knuckled drive
to emergency

SUSAN FARNER

winter storm
she crosses to the church
with her walker

BISWAJIT MISHRA

super cyclone
the slum temple upturned
with the banyan

STEFFIE GROW

the swollen river
swept along in the current
a child's red shoe

DEBORAH GUENTHER BEACHBOARD

power outage
only the sound of wind
to keep her company

TUYET VAN DO

heavy downpour
swimming in the town centre
crocodiles

JO ANNE MOSER GIBBONS

no Ark—
doe and buck
drown downstream

SRINIVASA RAO SAMBANGI

lighthouse
the depth of tsunami
by the faded color

DEBORAH A. BENNETT

awake at night
in howling wind
the sound of falling branches

MARIEL HERBERT

a dog's bark
expands in darkness
blackout

BRYAN RICKERT

power outage
the love making continues
by candlelight

ALLYSON WHIPPLE

early morning storm
waking to believe
it's still night

DAN SCHWERIN

metal roof
how the rain wants
to be remembered

JESSICA ALLYSON

muted thunder
goldfinches return
to our feeders

FRANK HIGGINS

earthquake
over the dark city
the stars brighter

MICHELE ROOT-BERNSTEIN

dregs of the storm trees torn from our roots

VALORIE BROADHURST WOERDEHOFF

the space between branches
where wind was
Hunter's Moon

CHRISTIANA DOUCETTE

sudden downpour
emptying the fridge and freezer
into the garbage

JACOB BLUMNER

floodwaters
family photos
cling together

SANDRA RIVERS-GILL

changing locations
for twelve lanterned nights
the power of prayer

JULIE BLOSS KELSEY

flooded highway
a great blue heron
in the cornfield

SARAH PARIS

storm drain
swept aside a tiny
pink sock

SCOTT WIGGERMAN

books embedded
with sand and grit
tornado-forced

SANDRA MARTYRES

inverted umbrellas
float on the flood waters—
deserted village

EDWARD CODY HUDDLESTON

where
the treeline was
breaking dawn

Memorial Day—
the rapid snowmelt river
down state street

CEÓ RUAÍRC

receding storm
so many heroes
flooding in

NITU YUMNAM

as if the rain wasn't loud enough the roof leak

MARIEL HERBERT

essential worker
a yellow beetle drives
through floodwater

CHARLES ROSSITER

oatmeal and chess
on the middle school gym floor
late summer hurricane

JASON GERRISH

listing their neighbors
to search and rescue...
floodwater debris

M. R. DEFIBAUGH

roll call...
too many moments of silence
after the cyclone

SHELLY RODRIGUE

empty houses...
black spray paint Xs
numbering the dead

RANDY BROOKS

upright piano
rests on the kitchen table
a flood survivor

VALORIE BROADHURST WOERDEHOFF

tree uprooted by a storm
the need to hold on
to something of yours

GORAN GATALICA

after snowmelt
a stream of cars
flooding the city

JILLIAN CALAHAN

still life—
flowers suspended
beneath water

JO ANNE MOSER GIBBONS

flooded barnyard...
vultures circling
remains of the livestock

ERIN CASTALDI

morning chill
the day awash
in storm debris

JOSHUA ST. CLAIRE

all day rain
a nameless bird flies off into
where the mountains were

SARAH PARIS

after the storm
a skeleton tree cradles
dawn

KIM KLUGH

receding flood waters
revealing the roots
of a town's resilience

JOHN PAPPAS

snowbound the light from a neighbor's house

DEBBIE STRANGE

aftermath
we tuck a note inside
the riven oak

SCOTT WIGGERMAN

sunlight
where trees once stood
our new view

JESSICA ALLYSON

after the deluge
last load of sleeping bags
in the dryer

RANDY BROOKS

floodwaters gone
the softness of mud left
over everything

WILBERT SALGADO

tornado after-math
our talk revolves around
what was insured

DEBORAH A. BENNETT

to abide nowhere
to be the owner of nothing
crescent moon

78

outage numbers long enough to dial my anxie

JILLIAN CALAHAN

day six
without power—
new president

GORDON BROWN

full garden pail
all that's left
of last week's hurricane

OLGA TRUBETSKOY

uprooted oaks
barricading the shore...
morning chainsaws

RANDY BROOKS

a carpet of muck
throughout the first floor
the smell of shit

ROB MCKINNON

receded flood...
the insides of homes
sodden on footpaths

how to prepare
for what has never happened
disappeared roads

M. R. DEFIBAUGH

reciting scripture
downed trees block
a muddled passage

LINDA CONROY

storm-soaked...
old women carried
from the rubble

on the front porch
drying in the sun
what's left

LORI BECHERER

after the flood
that innocent glimmer
of sunlight

EDWARD CODY HUDDLESTON

power lines sagging the wait of the world

JULIE SCHWERIN

thistledown
a comprehension of gone
taking root

KENDALL LOTT

a little girl
cuddles her kitten
rescue boat

RICH SCHILLING

homeless
for now
wind blown seeds

CURT LINDERMAN

every late august
the memories land
Katrina

BRYAN RICKERT

in the storm's wake
crawfish rebuilding
their chimneys

BAISALI CHATTERJEE DUTT

relief package
her pet cat
comes home

disaster coverage—
a family heirloom
found in the silt

JOSHUA ST. CLAIRE

sharps and flats
robinsong
after the derecho

SUSAN BETH FURST

assembling relief kits
in the church basement
His hands and feet

FRANK HIGGINS

after the flood
a robin adds a shoestring
to the new nest

JUDIT HOLLOS

storm shelter
a surviving family
starts life from scratch

SUZANNE TYRPAK

after the rain...
the world holds its breath
before sparrows sing

BETSY HEARNE

coastal pine
the twisting winds
we survive

ACKNOWLEDGEMENTS

Randy Brooks
"upright piano," *Bamboo Hut* 1
"a carpet of muck," *Under the Basho,*
March 22, 2023

Eric Burke
"lifting a snake," *Modern Haiku* 51.

Deborah A. Bennett
"awake at night," *Scarlet Dragonfly
Journal,* October 2022
"to abide nowhere," *Trash Panda
Haiku,* Summer 2023

M. R. Defibaugh
"roll call...," *Trash Panda,* Summer
2022
"reciting scripture," *Haiku in Action,*
December 24, 2021

Ben Gaa
"cicadas," *Notes from the Gean* 3:2

Goran Gatalica
"after snowmelt," *tsuri-dōrō,*
March/April 2024

Frank Higgins
"after the flood," *on Earth as it is*
(Spartan Press)
"earthquake," *on Earth as it is*
(Spartan Press)

"tree uprooted by a storm," *Modern Haiku* 52.1

www.ingramcontent.com/pod-product-compliance
Lightning Source LLC
Chambersburg PA
CBHW040541170726
48295CB00012B/545